DOG ON A LOG™
Chapter Books
Step 1

This is a work of fiction. Names, characters, places, and incidents are either products of the author's imagination or are used fictitiously. Any resemblance to actual persons, living or dead, businesses, companies, events, or locales is entirely coincidental.

DOG ON A LOG Books
Tucson, Arizona

Public Domain images from
www.clker.com

ISBN: 978-1949471113

Library of Congress Control Number:
2020901600

www.dogonalogbooks.com

DOG ON A LOG
Parent and Teacher Guides

General information
on Dyslexia and
Struggling Readers

The Author's Routine
for Teaching Reading

Book 1. *Teaching a Struggling Reader: One Mom's Experience with Dyslexia*

Book 2. *How to Use Decodable Books to Teach Reading*

Available for free from many online booksellers or read at:
www.dogonalogbooks.com/free

Download DOG ON A LOG printable gameboards, games, flashcards, and other activities at:
www.dogonalogbooks.com/printables.

Parents and Teachers:
Receive email notifications of new books and printables. Sign up at:
www.dogonalogbooks.com/subscribe

THE DOG
ON THE LOG

DOG ON A LOG Chapter Books
Step 1

By Pamela Brookes

A Bit of a Pup

The dog is on a log. He is a bit of a dog. He is a pup.

The pup has a kid. His kid is a gal. His kid is Jan.

The dog is on a log.

To the Dam

"Tup," Jan says to the dog. "You are my pup. Let us hop."

Tup does wag.

"Let us go to the dam," Jan says.

They hop and run and hop to the dam. The sun is hot. Jan is hot. Tup is hot.

Jan is Wet

At the dam, Jan says, "Let us get wet."

Hop, hop, hop. Jan is wet.

Tup does not want to get wet. He does not like to be wet. He can see Jan is wet and she is OK.

Jan is wet.

Tup is Wet

Tup's leg is wet. He does not like that. Hop! Hop to the rock. His leg is not wet.

"You are OK. It is OK to be wet. You can get wet," Jan says.

Tup's back leg is wet. He does not like to be wet.

Tup's back leg is wet. He does not like to be wet.

"You are OK," Jan says.

Jan is wet. Her leg is wet. Her back is wet. Her neck is wet. She is OK.

If Jan can get wet, Tup can get wet. He does not want to get wet.

The Fish

Tup can see a fish. It is a big fish. A big red fish. Hop, hop, hop, to the fish. His leg is wet. His back is wet. His chin is wet. His neck is wet. He is wet, wet, wet.

This is fun!

He is wet, wet, wet. This is fun!

Hop, hop, hop to Jan. She is wet. Tup is wet. The big red fish is wet.

This is fun!

A pup.

A dog.

Sight Words used in
"THE DOG ON THE LOG"

a, are, be, does, go, goes, has, he, her, his, into, is, like, my, of, OK, says, see, she, the, they, to, want, you

Approximately 260 total words

KEYWORDS
Alphabet

Aa	Bb
apple	bat
Cc	Dd
cat	dog

Ee	Ff
Ed	fun
Gg	Hh
game	hat
Ii	Jj
itch	jug

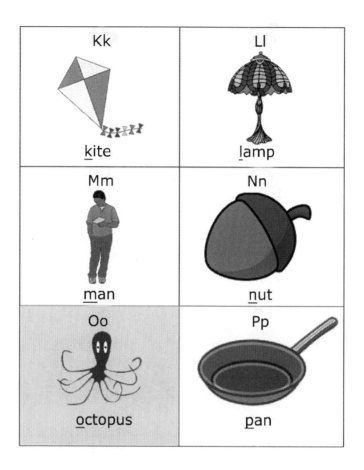

Kk	Ll
kite	lamp
Mm	Nn
man	nut
Oo	Pp
octopus	pan

Qu qu  <u>qu</u>een	Rr <u>r</u>at
Ss <u>s</u>nake	Tt <u>t</u>op
Uu <u>u</u>p	Vv <u>v</u>an

Ww	Xx
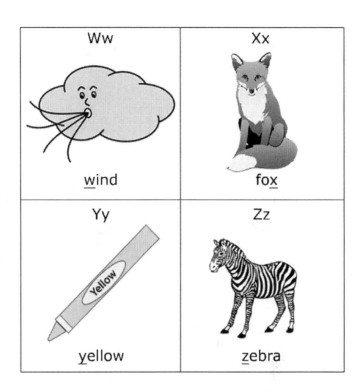	
<u>w</u>ind	fo<u>x</u>
Yy	Zz
<u>y</u>ellow	<u>z</u>ebra

Digraphs

ch	sh
chin	ship
th	th
thumb	mother
wh	-ck
whistle	sock

DOG ON A LOG Books
Phonics Progression

DOG ON A LOG Pup Books
Book 1
Phonological/Phonemic Awareness:
- Words
- Rhyming
- Syllables, identification, blending, segmenting
- Identifying individual letter sounds

Books 2-3
Phonemic Awareness/Phonics
- Consonants, primary sounds
- Short vowels
- Blending
- Introduction to sight words

DOG ON A LOG Let's GO! and Chapter Books

Step 1
- Consonants, primary sounds
- Short vowels
- Digraphs: ch, sh, th, wh, ck
- 2 and 3 sound words
- Possessive 's

Step 2
- Bonus letters (f, l, s, z after short vowel)
- "all"
- –s suffix

Step 3
- Letter Buddies: ang, ing, ong, ung, ank, ink, onk, unk

Step 4
- Consonant blends to make 4 sound words
- 3 and 4 sound words ending in –lk, -sk

Step 5
- Digraph blend –nch to make 3 and 4 sound words
- Silent e, including "-ke"

Step 6
- Exception words containing: ild, old, olt, ind, ost

Step 7
- 5 sounds in a closed syllable word plus suffix -s (crunch, slumps)
- 3 letter blends and up to 6 sounds in a closed syllable word (script, spring)

Step 8

- Two-syllable words with 2 closed syllables, not blends (sunset, chicken, unlock)

Step 9

- Two-syllable words with all previously introduced sounds including blends, exception words, and silent "e" (blacksmith, kindness, inside)
- Vowel digraphs: ai, ay, ea, ee, ie, oa, oe (rain, play, beach, tree, pie, boat, toe)

WATCH FOR MORE STEPS COMING SOON

Let's GO! Books have less text

Chapter Books are longer

DOG ON A LOG Books
Sight Word Progression

DOG ON A LOG Pup Books
a, does, go, has, her is, of, says, the, to

DOG ON A LOG Let's GO! and
Chapter Books

Step 1
a, and, are, be, does, go, goes, has, he, her, his, into, is, like, my, of, OK, says, see, she, the, they, to, want, you

Step 2
could, do, eggs, for, from, have, here, I, likes, me, nest, onto, or, puts, said, say, sees, should, wants, was, we, what, would, your

Step 3
as, Mr., Mrs., no, put, their, there, where

Step 4
push, saw

Step 5
come, comes, egg, pull, pulls, talk, walk, walks

Step 6
Ms., so, some, talks

Step 7
Hmmm, our, out, Pop E., TV

Step 8
Dr., friend, full, hi, island, people, please

More DOG ON A LOG Books

Most books available in Paperback, Hardback, and e-book formats

DOG ON A LOG Parent and Teacher Guides

Book 1 (Also in FREE e-book and PDF Bookfold)
- Teaching a Struggling Reader: One Mom's Experience with Dyslexia

Book 2 (FREE e-book and PDF Bookfold only)
- How to Use Decodable Books to Teach Reading

DOG ON A LOG Pup Books
Book 1
- Before the Squiggle Code (A Roadmap to Reading)

Books 2-3
- The Squiggle Code (Letters Make Words)
- Kids' Squiggles (Letters Make Words)

DOG ON A LOG Let's GO! and Chapter Books

Step 1
- The Dog on the Log
- The Pig Hat
- Chad the Cat
- Zip the Bug
- The Fish and the Pig

Step 2
- Mud on the Path
- The Red Hen
- The Hat and Bug Shop
- Babs the 'Bot
- The Cub

Step 3
- Mr. Bing has Hen Dots
- The Junk Lot Cat
- Bonk Punk Hot Rod
- The Ship with Wings
- The Sub in the Fish Tank

Step 4
- The Push Truck
- The Sand Hill
- Lil Tilt and Mr. Ling
- Musk Ox in the Tub
- The Trip to the Pond

Step 5
- Bake a Cake
- The Crane at the Cave
- Ride a Bike
- Crane or Crane?
- The Swing Gate

Step 6
- The Colt
- The Gold Bolt
- Hide in the Blinds
- The Stone Child
- Tolt the Kind Cat

Step 7
- Quest for A Grump Grunt
- The Blimp
- The Spring in the Lane
- Stamp for a Note
- Stripes and Splats

Step 8
- Anvil and Magnet
- The Mascot
- Kevin's Rabbit Hole
- The Humbug Vet and Medic Shop
- Chickens in the Attic

Step 9
- Trip to Cactus Gulch 1: The Step-Up Team
- Trip to Cactus Gulch 2: Into the Mineshaft
- Play the Bagpipes
- The Hidden Tale 1: The Lost Snapshot

All chapter books can be purchased individually or with all the same-step books in one volume.

Steps 1-5 can be bought as Let's GO! Books which are less text companions to the chapter books.

All titles can be bought as chapter books.

WATCH FOR MORE BOOKS COMING SOON

How You Can Help

Parents often worry that their child (or even adult learner) is not going to learn to read. Hearing other people's successes (especially when they struggled) can give worried parents or teachers hope. I would encourage others to share their experiences with products you've used by posting reviews at your favorite bookseller(s) stating how your child benefitted from those books or materials (whether it was DOG ON A LOG Books or another book or product.) This will help other parents and teachers know which products they should consider using. More than that, hearing your successes could truly help another family feel hopeful. It's amazing that something as seemingly small as a review can ease someone's concerns.

DOG ON A LOG Quick Assessment

Have your child read the following words. If they can't read every word in a Step, that is probably where in the series they should start. Get a printable assessment sheet at: www.dogonalogbooks.com/how-to-use/assessment-tool/

Step 1
fin, mash, sock, sub, cat, that, Dan's

Step 2
less, bats, tell, mall, chips, whiff, falls

Step 3
bangs, dank, honk, pings, chunk, sink, gong, rungs

Step 4
silk, fluff, smash, krill, drop, slim, whisk

Step 5
hunch, crate, rake, tote, inch, mote, lime

Step 6
child, molts, fold, hind, jolt, post, colds

Step 7
strive, scrape, splint, twists, crunch, prints, blend

Step 8
finish, denim, within, bathtub, laptop, medic, habit

Step 9
hundred, goldfinch, free, wheat, inhale, play, Joe

Made in United States
Orlando, FL
24 March 2024

45120342R00024